Contents

Animal Planet

Hedgehogs

1 package (about 18 ounces) chocolate cake mix, plus ingredients to prepare mix
1 container (16 ounces) chocolate frosting
Black jelly beans
Small round white candies
Black decorating gel
Candy-coated licorice pieces

1. Preheat oven to 350°F. Place 22 standard (2-inch) silicone muffin cups on large baking sheet or line 22 standard (2½-inch) muffin cups with paper baking cups.

2. Prepare cake mix according to package directions. Spoon batter into prepared muffin cups, filling two-thirds full.

3. Bake 18 to 22 minutes or until toothpick inserted into centers comes out clean. If using muffin pans, cool cupcakes in pans 10 minutes; remove to wire racks to cool completely.

4. Frost cupcakes. Cut jelly beans in half crosswise for noses. Arrange jelly bean halves and round candies on one side of each cupcake to create faces; pipe dot of decorating gel onto each eye. Arrange licorice pieces around face and all over each cupcake. *Makes 22 cupcakes*

Colorful Caterpillar Cupcakes

1 package (about 18 ounces) vanilla cake mix
1¼ cups water
3 eggs
⅓ cup vegetable oil
Assorted food coloring
1 container (16 ounces) white frosting
Assorted candies, candy-coated chocolate pieces, red string licorice and lollipops
Gummy worms

1. Preheat oven to 350°F. Line 22 standard (2½-inch) muffin cups with paper baking cups.*

2. Beat cake mix, water, eggs and oil in large bowl with electric mixer at low speed 30 seconds. Beat at medium speed 2 minutes or until well blended. Divide batter between five bowls; add food coloring to batter, a few drops at a time, until desired shades are reached. Spoon batter into prepared muffin cups, filling two-thirds full.

3. Bake 16 to 18 minutes or until toothpick inserted into centers comes out clean. Cool cupcakes in pans 10 minutes; remove to wire racks to cool completely.

4. Set aside two cupcakes for caterpillar head. Frost remaining cupcakes. Place one cupcake on its side towards one end of serving platter. Place second cupcake on its side next to first cupcake; arrange remaining cupcakes, alternating colors, in row to create body of caterpillar.

5. Frost one reserved cupcake; decorate with assorted candies, chocolate pieces, licorice and lollipops to create face. Place plain cupcake upright at front of cupcake row for head; top with face cupcake on its side. Cut gummy worms into small pieces; attach to caterpillar body with frosting to create legs.

Makes 22 cupcakes

**Use white paper baking cups to best show colors of caterpillar.*

Colorful Caterpillar Cupcakes

Dinocakes

1 package (about 18 ounces) chocolate fudge or devil's food cake mix, plus ingredients to prepare mix
44 long chewy chocolate candies (3×¼ inch), divided
10 to 15 small chewy chocolate candies
1 container (16 ounces) chocolate frosting
Candy sprinkles and decorating decors

1. Preheat oven to 350°F. Line 22 standard (2½-inch) muffin cups with paper baking cups.

2. Prepare cake mix according to package directions. Spoon batter into prepared muffin cups, filling two-thirds full.

3. Bake 18 to 22 minutes or until toothpick inserted into centers comes out clean. Cool cupcakes in pans 10 minutes; remove to wire racks to cool completely.

4. Shape 22 long candies into dinosaur heads. (If candies are too stiff to bend, heat in microwave on LOW (30%) 6 to 8 seconds to soften.)

5. Cut about 1 inch from remaining 22 long candies with scissors; shape each into pointed tail. Make 4 to 5 small cuts along length of candies, being careful not to cut all the way through. Curve candies into tail shape. Press and flatten small candies into rectangles; cut rectangles into small triangles for dinosaur spikes.

6. Frost cupcakes. Press candy head and tail into opposite sides of each cupcake; arrange candy triangles in between. Decorate with sprinkles; press decors into dinosaur heads for eyes. *Makes 22 cupcakes*

Dinocakes

Little Lamb Cakes

1 package (about 18 ounces) yellow cake mix, plus ingredients to prepare mix
1 container (16 ounces) vanilla frosting
15 large marshmallows
Pink jelly beans or decorating candies
1 package (10½ ounces) mini marshmallows
Black string licorice
44 mini chocolate chips

1. Preheat oven to 350°F. Line 22 standard (2½-inch) muffin cups with paper baking cups.

2. Prepare cake mix according to package directions. Spoon batter into prepared muffin cups, filling two-thirds full.

3. Bake 18 to 22 minutes or until toothpick inserted into centers comes out clean. Cool cupcakes in pans 10 minutes; remove to wire racks to cool completely.

4. Frost cupcakes. Cut each large marshmallow crosswise into 3 pieces. Stretch pieces into oval shapes; arrange on cupcakes to resemble ears. Attach pink jelly bean to each ear with frosting.

5. Press mini marshmallows into frosting around edge of cupcakes. Cut jelly beans in half crosswise; cut licorice into ½-inch pieces. Create faces with mini chips for eyes, half jelly bean for noses and licorice for mouths.

Makes 22 cupcakes

Little Lamb Cakes

Mini Mice

1 package (about 18 ounces) chocolate cake mix, plus ingredients to prepare mix
1 container (16 ounces) chocolate frosting
1 cup white frosting (optional)
Small black and pink hard candies or decors
Small fruit-flavored pastel candy wafers
Black string licorice

1. Preheat oven to 350°F. Line 60 mini (1¾-inch) muffin cups with paper baking cups.

2. Prepare cake mix according to package directions. Spoon batter into prepared muffin cups, filling almost full.

3. Bake about 12 minutes or until toothpick inserted into centers comes out clean. Cool cupcakes in pans 10 minutes; remove to wire racks to cool completely.

4. For brown mice, frost cupcakes with chocolate frosting; use knife or small spatula to pull up frosting and create fuzzy appearance. For speckled mice, frost cupcakes with white frosting; use toothpick to add streaks of chocolate frosting.

5. Arrange candies on one side of each cupcake to create eyes, nose and ears. Cut licorice into 3-inch lengths; press into opposite end of each cupcake to create tail.

Makes 60 mini cupcakes

Mini Mice

Panda Cupcakes

- 1 package (about 18 ounces) yellow cake mix, plus ingredients to prepare mix
- 1 container (16 ounces) vanilla frosting
- Large chocolate nonpareil candies or chocolate discs*
- Small chocolate nonpareil candies
- 8 ounces semisweet chocolate, chopped *or* 1½ cups semisweet chocolate chips
- White candy sprinkles
- Red jelly beans

**Chocolate discs are available at many gourmet, craft and baking supply stores. Large chocolate nonpareil candies may be substituted.*

1. Preheat oven to 350°F. Line 22 standard (2½-inch) muffin cups with paper baking cups.

2. Prepare cake mix according to package directions. Spoon batter into prepared muffin cups, filling two-thirds full.

3. Bake 18 to 22 minutes or until toothpick inserted into centers comes out clean. Cool cupcakes in pans 10 minutes; remove to wire racks to cool completely.

4. Frost cupcakes. Arrange two large chocolate candies on edge of each cupcake for ears. Attach one nonpareil candy to each ear with frosting.

5. Place semisweet chocolate in small food storage bag. Microwave on HIGH about 1½ minutes or until chocolate is melted, kneading bag every 30 seconds. Cut very small hole in corner of bag; pipe kidney shapes for eyes. Place candy sprinkle on each eye. Place jelly bean between eyes for nose. Pipe mouth with melted chocolate. *Makes 22 cupcakes*

Panda Cupcakes

Chocolate Moose

- 1 package (about 18 ounces) chocolate cake mix, plus ingredients to prepare mix
- 1 container (16 ounces) milk chocolate frosting
- ½ to ¾ cup vanilla frosting
- 1 package (12 ounces) semisweet chocolate chips
- 2 tablespoons shortening
- White round candies
- Small black candies
- Black decorating gel
- Pretzel twists

1. Preheat oven to 350°F. Line 22 standard (2½-inch) muffin cups with paper baking cups.

2. Prepare cake mix according to package directions. Spoon batter into prepared muffin cups, filling two-thirds full.

3. Bake 18 to 22 minutes or until toothpick inserted into centers comes out clean. Cool cupcakes in pans 10 minutes; remove to wire racks to cool completely.

4. Combine chocolate frosting and ½ cup vanilla frosting in medium bowl until well blended. (Stir in additional vanilla frosting for lighter color.) Frost cupcakes.

5. Place chocolate chips and shortening in medium microwavable bowl. Microwave on HIGH 1½ minutes or until chocolate is melted and mixture is smooth, stirring every 30 seconds. Place chocolate in pastry bag or small food storage bag with small corner cut off. Pipe chocolate mixture into shape of moose head on each cupcake as shown in photo; smooth chocolate with small spatula. (Chocolate may need to be reheated slightly if it becomes too stiff to pipe.)

6. Arrange candies on cupcakes to create eyes and noses. Pipe small dot of decorating gel or chocolate mixture onto each eye. Break off small section of each pretzel twist to form antlers. Push ends of pretzels into top of cupcakes.

Makes 22 cupcakes

Chocolate Moose

Fishy Friends

1 package (about 18 ounces) cake mix, any flavor, plus ingredients to prepare mix
1 container (16 ounces) white frosting
Orange, purple and blue food coloring
Assorted color jelly candy fruit slices
Colored round gummy candies
White round candies
Black decorating gel

1. Preheat oven to 350°F. Line 22 standard (2½-inch) muffin cups with paper baking cups.

2. Prepare cake mix according to package directions. Spoon batter into prepared muffin cups, filling two-thirds full.

3. Bake 18 to 22 minutes or until toothpick inserted into centers comes out clean. Cool cupcakes in pans 10 minutes; remove to wire racks to cool completely.

4. Divide frosting between three small bowls. Add food coloring, a few drops at a time, until desired shades are reached. Frost cupcakes.

5. Cut jelly candies into triangles for fins and tails. Arrange white candies and gummy candies at one end of each cupcake to create faces; add dot of decorating gel to each eye. Arrange jelly candy triangles on top and side of each cupcake.

Makes 22 cupcakes

Fishy Friends

Tasty Turtles

1 package (about 18 ounces) chocolate cake mix, plus ingredients to prepare mix
1½ packages (12 ounces each) small chewy chocolate candies
Green food coloring
1 container (16 ounces) vanilla frosting
Chocolate-covered raisins, chocolate chips or candy-coated chocolate pieces
White decorating decors

1. Preheat oven to 350°F. Line 22 standard (2½-inch) muffin cups with paper baking cups.

2. Prepare cake mix according to package directions. Spoon batter into prepared muffin cups, filling two-thirds full.

3. Bake 18 to 22 minutes or until toothpick inserted into centers comes out clean. Cool cupcakes in pans 10 minutes; remove to wire racks to cool completely.

4. For each turtle, cut two candies in half; shape pieces into feet. Shape one candy into turtle head. (To soften candies for easier shaping, microwave on LOW (30%) 6 to 8 seconds.) Stretch one candy into long thin rope; cut into ½-inch pieces for turtle tails.

5. Remove paper baking cups; cut off ½ inch from bottom of each cupcake. Add food coloring to frosting in small bowl, a few drops at a time, until desired shade of green is reached. Frost tops of cupcakes.

6. Press candy head and tail into opposite ends of each cupcake; press chocolate-covered raisins into frosting. Press decors into head for eyes. Arrange four candy feet around each turtle. *Makes 22 cupcakes*

Tasty Turtles

Monkey A-Rounds

1 package (about 18 ounces) chocolate cake mix, plus ingredients to prepare mix
1 container (16 ounces) chocolate frosting
1 container (16 ounces) white frosting
Yellow food coloring
Chocolate discs
Small black jelly beans
Black string licorice

1. Preheat oven to 350°F. Line 22 standard (2½-inch) muffin cups with paper baking cups.

2. Prepare cake mix according to package directions. Spoon batter into prepared muffin cups, filling two-thirds full.

3. Bake 18 to 22 minutes or until toothpick inserted into centers comes out clean. Cool cupcakes in pans 10 minutes; remove to wire racks to cool completely.

4. Frost cupcakes with chocolate frosting. Place white frosting in small bowl. Add food coloring, a few drops at a time, until desired shade of yellow is reached. Transfer frosting to pastry bag or small food storage bag with small corner cut off.

5. Pipe circle of yellow frosting in center of each chocolate disc for ears. Cut jelly beans in half crosswise for eyes; cut licorice into smaller lengths for mouths and noses. Pipe yellow frosting into oval shape on each cupcake as shown in photo; arrange eyes just above oval and ears on either side of cupcake. Arrange licorice noses and mouths inside oval. Use toothpick or knife to pull up frosting at top of cupcake into hair (or use pastry bag with special tip to pipe hair). *Makes 22 cupcakes*

Monkey A-Rounds

Princess Power

Fairy Tale Cupcakes

1 package (about 18 ounces) cake mix, any flavor, plus ingredients to prepare mix
1 container (16 ounces) white frosting
Pink, purple , blue and yellow food coloring
Silver dragees
Assorted decoratifs and decors

1. Preheat oven to 350°F. Line 22 standard (2½-inch) muffin cups with paper baking cups or spray with nonstick cooking spray.

2. Prepare cake mix according to package directions. Spoon batter into prepared muffin cups, filling two-thirds full.

3. Bake 18 to 22 minutes or until toothpick inserted into centers comes out clean. Cool cupcakes in pans 10 minutes; remove to wire racks to cool completely.

4. Divide frosting between four bowls; add different food coloring to each bowl, a few drops at a time, until desired shades are reached. Frost cupcakes with pink, purple and blue frosting; smooth tops with small spatula.

5. Spoon yellow frosting into pastry bag with round decorating tip or small food storage bag with small corner cut off. Pipe crowns and wands on cupcakes; decorate with dragees, decoratifs and decors.

Makes 22 cupcakes

Marshmallow Delights

2 cups all-purpose flour
1 teaspoon baking soda
1 teaspoon baking powder
½ teaspoon salt
½ cup sour cream
½ cup milk
1 teaspoon vanilla
1 cup granulated sugar
½ cup (1 stick) butter, softened
2 eggs
1½ cups white frosting
Green food coloring
3 cups fruit-flavored mini marshmallows
Green sparkling sugar

1. Preheat oven to 350°F. Line 12 standard (2½-inch) muffin cups with paper baking cups. Sift flour, baking soda, baking powder and salt into medium bowl. Combine sour cream, milk and vanilla in small bowl until well blended.

2. Beat granulated sugar and butter in large bowl with electric mixer at medium speed 2 minutes or until fluffy. Add eggs, one at a time, beating well after each addition. Add flour mixture alternately with sour cream mixture, beginning and ending with flour mixture, beating well after each addition. Spoon batter evenly into prepared muffin cups.

3. Bake 21 to 23 minutes or until toothpick inserted into centers comes out clean. Cool cupcakes in pan 5 minutes; remove to wire rack to cool completely.

4. Place frosting in small bowl. Add food coloring, a few drops at a time, until desired shade of green is reached. Frost cupcakes. Arrange marshmallows over frosting; sprinkle with sparkling sugar.

Makes 12 cupcakes

Marshmallow Delights

Butterfly Cupcakes

1 package (about 18 ounces) cake mix, any flavor, plus ingredients to prepare mix
1 container (16 ounces) white frosting
Blue and green food coloring
Colored sugar and sparkling sugar
Candy-coated chocolate pieces
Red string licorice , cut into 4-inch pieces

1. Preheat oven to 350°F. Lightly spray 22 standard (2½-inch) muffin cups with nonstick cooking spray.

2. Prepare cake mix according to package directions. Spoon batter into prepared muffin cups, filling two-thirds full.

3. Bake 18 to 22 minutes or until toothpick inserted into centers comes out clean. Cool cupcakes in pans 10 minutes; remove to wire racks to cool completely.

4. Divide frosting between two small bowls. Add one color food coloring to each bowl, one drop at a time, until desired shades of blue and green are reached.

5. Cut cupcakes in half vertically. Frost cupcake halves. Place halves together, cut sides out, to resemble butterfly wings; decorate with colored sugar, sparkling sugar and chocolate pieces. Snip each end of licorice pieces to form antennae; place in center of each cupcake.

Makes 22 cupcakes

Butterfly Cupcakes

Angelic Cupcakes

1 package (about 16 ounces) angel food cake mix
1¼ cups cold water
¼ teaspoon peppermint extract (optional)
Red food coloring
4½ cups whipped topping

1. Preheat oven to 375°F. Line 36 standard (2½-inch) muffin cups with paper baking cups.

2. Beat cake mix, water and peppermint extract, if desired, in large bowl with electric mixer at low speed 2 minutes. Pour half of batter into medium bowl; fold in 9 drops food coloring. Alternate spoonfuls of white and pink batter in each prepared muffin cup, filling three-fourths full.

3. Bake 11 minutes or until cupcakes are golden brown with deep cracks on top. Remove to wire racks to cool completely.

4. Divide whipped topping between two small bowls. Add 2 drops red food coloring to one bowl; stir gently until whipped topping is evenly colored. Frost cupcakes with pink and white whipped topping as desired.

Makes 36 cupcakes

Tip Pink food coloring is available at specialty baking and craft stores; it can be used instead of red. You may need to add more than the recipe directs to reach the desired shade of pink.

Angelic Cupcakes

Friendly Frogs

1 package (about 18 ounces) cake mix, any flavor, plus ingredients to prepare mix
1 container (16 ounces) white frosting
Green food coloring
Green sparkling sugar (optional)
Black round candies or candy-coated chocolate pieces
White chocolate candy discs
Black and red string licorice
Green jelly candy fruit slices

1. Preheat oven to 350°F. Line 22 standard (2½-inch) muffin cups with paper baking cups.

2. Prepare cake mix according to package directions. Spoon batter into prepared muffin cups, filling two-thirds full.

3. Bake 18 to 22 minutes or until toothpick inserted into centers comes out clean. Cool cupcakes in pans 10 minutes; remove to wire racks to cool completely.

4. Place frosting in small bowl. Add food coloring, a few drops at a time, until desired shade of green is reached. Frost cupcakes; sprinkle with sparkling sugar, if desired.

5. Use small dab of frosting to attach black candies to white discs for eyes. Cut licorice into smaller lengths for mouths and noses. Arrange candies on cupcakes to create frog faces.

6. Use scissors to cut jelly candies into feet, if desired. Set cupcakes on candy feet when ready to serve.

Makes 22 cupcakes

Friendly Frogs

Under the Sea

- 1 package (about 18 ounces) cake mix, any flavor, plus ingredients to prepare mix
- 2 containers (16 ounces each) white frosting
- Blue, green, yellow, red and purple food coloring
- White sparkling sugar (optional)
- Black decorating gel
- Assorted color decors, nonpareils and candy fish

1. Preheat oven to 350°F. Line 22 standard (2½-inch) muffin cups with paper baking cups or spray with nonstick cooking spray.

2. Prepare cake mix according to package directions. Spoon batter into prepared muffin cups, filling two-thirds full.

3. Bake 18 to 22 minutes or until toothpick inserted into centers comes out clean. Cool cupcakes in pans 10 minutes; remove to wire racks to cool completely.

4. Place frosting from one container in medium bowl; add blue and green food coloring, a few drops at a time, until desired shade of aqua is reached. Spoon into pastry bag with large star decorating tip. Pipe frosting in swirl pattern on cupcakes. Sprinkle with sparkling sugar, if desired.

5. Divide remaining frosting between four small bowls; add different food coloring (except blue) to each bowl, a few drops at a time, until desired shades are reached. Spoon each color into pastry bags with round decorating tip or food storage bags with small corner cut off. Pipe sea creatures and plants on cupcakes: yellow fish, red lobsters, purple starfish and green seaweed. Decorate with decorating gel, decors and candies.

Makes 22 cupcakes

Under the Sea

Pretty in Pink

2 cups all-purpose flour
1 teaspoon baking soda
1 teaspoon baking powder
½ teaspoon salt
½ cup sour cream
½ cup milk
1 teaspoon vanilla
1 cup granulated sugar
½ cup (1 stick) butter, softened
2 eggs
2 to 3 tablespoons multi-colored cake decors (sprinkles)
Pink food coloring
1 container (16 ounces) white frosting
12 small tiaras
White and pink sparkling sugars

1. Preheat oven to 350°F. Line 12 standard (2½-inch) muffin cups with paper baking cups. Sift flour, baking soda, baking powder and salt into medium bowl. Combine sour cream, milk and vanilla in small bowl until well blended.

2. Beat granulated sugar and butter in large bowl with electric mixer at medium speed 2 minutes or until fluffy. Add eggs, one at a time, beating well after each addition. Add flour mixture alternately with sour cream mixture, beginning and ending with flour mixture, beating well after each addition. Stir in decors until blended. Spoon batter evenly into prepared muffin cups.

3. Bake 21 to 23 minutes or until toothpick inserted into centers comes out clean. Cool cupcakes in pan 5 minutes; remove to wire rack to cool completely.

4. Stir food coloring into frosting in small bowl, a few drops at a time, until desired shade of pink is reached. Pipe or spread frosting on cupcakes. Arrange tiaras on cupcakes; sprinkle with sparkling sugars.

Makes 12 cupcakes

Pretty in Pink

Dragonflies

1 package (about 18 ounces) cake mix, any flavor, plus ingredients to prepare mix
White confectionary coating*
Pink, purple, yellow and green food coloring
44 small pretzel twists
22 pretzel sticks (about 3 inches)
1 container (16 ounces) white frosting
White and purple nonpareils
Silver dragees

**Confectionery coating, also called almond bark or candy coating, can be found at craft stores and in the baking section of the supermarket. It comes in blocks, discs and chips and is usually available in white, milk and dark chocolate varieties.*

1. Preheat oven to 350°F. Line 22 standard (2½-inch) muffin cups with paper baking cups.

2. Prepare cake mix according to package directions. Spoon batter into prepared muffin cups, filling two-thirds full.

3. Bake 18 to 22 minutes or until toothpick inserted into centers comes out clean. Cool cupcakes in pans 10 minutes; remove to wire racks to cool completely.

4. Line large baking sheet with waxed paper. Melt confectionary coating according to package directions. Stir in pink food coloring, a few drops at a time, until desired shade of pink is reached. Dip pretzel twists in melted candy to coat; arrange two twists together on prepared baking sheet. Dip pretzel sticks in melted candy; place one stick between two pretzel twists to create dragonfly. Sprinkle pretzel twists with white nonpareils; arrange two purple nonpareils at top of pretzel sticks for eyes. Press dragees into bottom half of pretzel sticks. Let stand 10 minutes or until set.

5. Meanwhile, divide frosting between three bowls. Add different food coloring (except pink) to each bowl, a few drops at a time, until desired shades are reached. Pipe or spread frosting on cupcakes; top with dragonflies.

Makes 22 cupcakes

Dragonflies

Just Plain Fun

Sunny Side Upcakes

1 package (about 18 ounces) vanilla cake mix, plus ingredients to prepare mix
22 yellow chewy fruit candies
2 containers (16 ounces each) white frosting

1. Preheat oven to 350°F. Line 22 standard (2½-inch) muffin cups with paper baking cups.

2. Prepare cake mix according to package directions. Spoon batter into prepared muffin cups, filling two-thirds full.

3. Bake 18 to 22 minutes or until toothpick inserted into centers comes out clean. Cool cupcakes in pans 10 minutes; remove to wire racks to cool completely.

4. For each egg yolk, microwave candy on LOW (30%) 5 seconds or just until softened. Shape into ball; flatten slightly.

5. Place 1 cup frosting in small microwavable bowl; microwave on LOW (30%) 10 seconds or until softened. Working with one cupcake at a time, spoon about 2 tablespoons frosting in center of cupcake. Spread frosting toward edges of cupcake in uneven petal shapes to resemble egg white. Press candy into frosting in center of cupcake. Microwave additional frosting as needed.

Makes 22 cupcakes

Cookie in a Cupcake

1 package (16 ounces) refrigerated break-apart chocolate chip cookie dough (24 count), divided
2 cups all-purpose flour
½ cup unsweetened cocoa powder
1 teaspoon baking soda
½ teaspoon salt
½ cup (1 stick) butter, softened
1 cup sugar
1 egg
1 teaspoon vanilla
½ cup sour cream
½ cup hot water

1. Preheat oven to 350°F. Place 12 standard (2-inch) silicone muffin cups on baking sheet or line 12 standard (2½-inch) muffin cups with paper baking cups.

2. Break apart half of cookie dough into 12 pieces along score lines. (Reserve remaining half of dough for another use.) Roll each piece of dough into a ball; refrigerate dough while preparing cupcake batter.

3. Sift flour, cocoa, baking soda and salt into medium bowl. Beat butter in large bowl with electric mixer about 2 minutes or until creamy. Add sugar; beat 2 to 3 minutes or until light and fluffy. Beat in egg until well blended. Beat in vanilla.

4. Add sour cream and water to butter mixture alternately with flour mixture, beginning and ending with flour mixture. Beat until blended. Spoon batter evenly into prepared muffin cups. Place 1 ball of cookie dough into each cup, pressing down into batter.

5. Bake 20 to 22 minutes or until toothpick inserted into cake portion of cupcake comes out clean. Cool cupcakes in pan 5 minutes; remove to wire rack to cool slightly. Serve warm. *Makes 12 cupcakes*

Cookie in a Cupcake

Hot Chocolate Cupcakes

1 package (about 16 ounces) pound cake mix, plus ingredients to prepare mix
4 containers (4 ounces each) prepared chocolate pudding*
2½ cups whipped topping, divided
4 small chewy chocolate candies
Unsweetened cocoa powder (optional)

**Or, purchase 1 (4-serving size) package instant chocolate pudding and pie filling mix and prepare according to package directions. Use 2 cups pudding for recipe; reserve remaining pudding for another use.*

1. Preheat oven to 350°F. Spray 15 standard (2½-inch) muffin cups with baking spray (nonstick cooking spray with flour added) or grease and flour cups.

2. Prepare cake mix according to package directions. Spoon batter into prepared muffin cups, filling about two-thirds full.

3. Bake 20 to 25 minutes or until toothpick inserted into centers comes out clean. Cool cupcakes in pans 5 minutes; remove to wire racks to cool completely.

4. Combine chocolate pudding and 2 cups whipped topping in medium bowl until well blended; refrigerate until ready to use.

5. Microwave chocolate candies on LOW (30%) 5 to 10 seconds or until slightly softened. Stretch each candy into long thin rope; cut ropes into 2-inch lengths. Curve candy pieces into "C" shape to create handles of mugs.

6. Cut out 2-inch circle about 1 inch deep from top of each cupcake with small paring knife. Cut two slits ½ inch apart with small paring knife in one side of each cupcake. Insert chocolate candy into slits to create mug handle. Fill hole in each cupcake with chocolate pudding mixture. Top with dollop of remaining whipped topping; sprinkle with cocoa, if desired.

Makes 15 cupcakes

Hot Chocolate Cupcakes

Marshmallow Fudge Sundae Cupcakes

1 package (about 18 ounces) chocolate cake mix, plus ingredients to prepare mix
2 packages (4 ounces each) waffle bowls
40 large marshmallows
1 jar (8 ounces) hot fudge topping
Colored sprinkles or chopped nuts
1¼ cups whipped topping
1 jar (10 ounces) maraschino cherries

1. Preheat oven to 350°F. Lightly spray 20 standard (2½-inch) muffin cups with nonstick cooking spray.

2. Prepare cake mix according to package directions. Spoon batter evenly into prepared muffin cups, filling two-thirds full.

3. Bake 18 to 22 minutes or until toothpick inserted into centers comes out clean. Cool cupcakes in pans 10 minutes; remove to wire racks to cool completely.

4. Place waffle bowls on ungreased baking sheets. Place one cupcake in each waffle bowl. Top each cupcake with 2 marshmallows; return to oven 2 minutes or until marshmallows are slightly softened.

5. Remove lid from hot fudge topping; microwave on HIGH 10 seconds or until softened. Top each cupcake with hot fudge topping, sprinkles, whipped topping and cherry. *Makes 20 cupcakes*

Marshmallow Fudge Sundae Cupcakes

Margarita Cupcakes

1 package (about 18 ounces) white cake mix
¾ cup plus 2 tablespoons margarita mix, divided
2 eggs
⅓ cup vegetable oil
¼ cup water
3 teaspoons grated lime peel (about 3 limes), divided
Juice of 1 lime
2 tablespoons tequila or lime juice
3 cups powdered sugar
1 tablespoon sparkling or granulated sugar
1 tablespoon salt (optional)
Green and yellow food coloring
Lime peel strips (optional)

1. Preheat oven to 350°F. Line 24 standard (2½-inch) muffin cups with paper baking cups.

2. Combine cake mix, ¾ cup margarita mix, eggs, oil, water, 1 teaspoon lime peel and lime juice in large bowl. Whisk 2 minutes or until well blended. Spoon batter evenly into prepared muffin cups.

3. Bake 20 to 25 minutes or until toothpick inserted into centers comes out clean. Cool cupcakes in pans 5 minutes; remove to wire racks to cool completely.

4. Combine tequila, remaining 2 tablespoons margarita mix and 2 teaspoons lime peel in medium bowl. Gradually whisk in powdered sugar until desired glaze consistency is reached. Combine sparkling sugar and salt, if desired, in small bowl. Add food coloring, one drop at a time, until desired shade of green is reached.

5. Spread glaze over cupcakes; dip edges in sugar-salt mixture. Garnish with lime peel strips.

Makes 24 cupcakes

Margarita Cupcakes

Quick Cookie Cupcakes

1 package (16 ounces) refrigerated break-apart chocolate chip cookie dough (24 count)
1½ cups chocolate frosting
Colored decors

1. Preheat oven to 350°F. Line 24 mini (1¾-inch) muffin cups with paper baking cups.

2. Break dough into 24 pieces along score lines. Roll each piece into a ball; place in prepared muffin cups.

3. Bake 10 to 12 minutes or until golden brown. Cool cupcakes in pans 5 minutes; remove to wire racks to cool completely.

4. Pipe or spread frosting over each cupcake. Sprinkle with decors.

Makes 24 mini cupcakes

Tip These cupcakes are perfect for every occasion—they can be made in just minutes, and you can change the paper baking cups and decorations to match your theme. Use pink colors for Valentine's Day; green for St. Patrick's Day; red, white and blue for the 4th of July; and school colors for graduation parties. Craft stores usually stock baking cups and cake decorations in seasonal colors and patterns.

Quick Cookie Cupcakes

Cupcake Sliders

2 cups all-purpose flour
2½ teaspoons baking powder
½ teaspoon salt
1 cup milk
½ teaspoon vanilla
1½ cups sugar
½ cup (1 stick) butter, softened
3 eggs
1¼ cups chocolate hazelnut spread or milk chocolate frosting
Colored decors (optional)

1. Preheat oven to 350°F. Spray 18 standard (2½-inch) muffin cups with nonstick cooking spray.

2. Combine flour, baking powder and salt in medium bowl. Combine milk and vanilla in measuring cup. Beat sugar and butter in large bowl with electric mixer at medium speed about 3 minutes or until creamy. Add eggs, one at a time, beating well after each addition. Add flour mixture alternately with milk mixture, beating until well blended. Spoon batter into prepared muffin cups, filling about three-fourths full.

3. Bake 18 to 20 minutes or until toothpick inserted into centers comes out clean. Cool cupcakes in pans 10 minutes; remove to wire racks to cool completely.

4. Cut off edges of cupcakes to form squares. Cut cupcakes in half crosswise. Spread each bottom half with about 1 tablespoon chocolate hazelnut spread; sprinkle with decors, if desired. Replace tops of cupcakes.

Makes 18 cupcakes

Cupcake Sliders

Surprise Package Cupcakes

1 package (about 18 ounces) cake mix, any flavor, plus ingredients to prepare mix
Food coloring
1 container (16 ounces) vanilla frosting
1 tube (4¼ ounces) white decorating icing
66 chewy fruit squares
Colored decors

1. Preheat oven to 350°F. Spray 22 standard (2½-inch) muffin cups with nonstick cooking spray or line with paper baking cups.

2. Prepare cake mix and bake in prepared muffin cups according to package directions. Cool cupcakes in pans 10 minutes; remove to wire racks to cool completely.

3. Add food coloring to frosting in small bowl, a few drops at a time, until desired shade is reached. Frost cupcakes.

4. Use icing to pipe ribbons on fruit squares to resemble wrapped presents. Place three candy presents on each cupcake. Decorate with decors.

Makes 22 cupcakes

Tip Use an ice cream scoop to fill the muffin cups with batter—it's quick, easy and helps keep the pans clean.

Surprise Package Cupcakes

Crispy Cupcakes

¼ cup (½ stick) plus 2 tablespoons butter, divided
1 package (10½ ounces) marshmallows
½ cup creamy peanut butter
6 cups crisp rice cereal
1 cup bittersweet or semisweet chocolate chips
1½ cups powdered sugar
¼ cup milk

1. Spray 13×9-inch baking pan with nonstick cooking spray. Microwave 2 tablespoons butter in large microwavable bowl on HIGH 30 seconds or until melted. Add marshmallows; stir until coated with butter. Microwave on HIGH 1 minute; stir. Microwave 45 seconds; stir until melted. Stir in peanut butter until well blended. Add cereal; stir until blended.

2. Spread mixture in prepared pan, using waxed paper to spread and press into even layer. Let stand 10 to 15 minutes until set.

3. Meanwhile, place remaining ¼ cup butter and chocolate chips in medium microwavable bowl. Microwave on HIGH 40 seconds; stir. Microwave at additional 15-second intervals until melted and smooth. Gradually beat in powdered sugar and milk until well blended. Refrigerate until ready to use.

4. Spray 1½-inch round cookie or biscuit cutter with nonstick cooking spray; cut out 36 circles from cereal bars. Place small dab of frosting on top of 18 circles; top with remaining 18 circles, pressing down firmly to seal. Place "cupcakes" in paper baking cups, if desired. Pipe or spread frosting on cupcakes.

Makes 18 cupcakes

Crispy Cupcakes

Peanut Butter & Jelly Cupcakes

1 package (about 18 ounces) yellow cake mix, plus ingredients to prepare mix
¾ cup creamy peanut butter
½ cup (1 stick) butter, softened
2 cups powdered sugar
½ teaspoon vanilla
¼ cup milk
2 cups strawberry jelly

1. Preheat oven to 350°F. Line 22 standard (2½-inch) muffin cups with paper baking cups.

2. Prepare cake mix according to package directions. Spoon batter into prepared muffin cups, filling two-thirds fill.

3. Bake 18 to 22 minutes or until toothpick inserted into centers comes out clean. Cool cupcakes in pans 10 minutes; remove to wire racks to cool completely.

4. Beat peanut butter and butter in medium bowl with electric mixer at medium speed 2 minutes or until smooth. Add sugar and vanilla; beat at low speed 1 minute or until crumbly. Slowly add milk, beating at low speed until creamy.

5. Fill pastry bag fitted with small decorator tip with jelly. Insert tip into top of cupcake; squeeze bag gently to fill center of cupcake with jelly. (Stop squeezing when you feel resistance or jelly comes out of top of cupcake.) Repeat with remaining cupcakes and jelly, refilling pastry bag as needed.

6. Pipe or spread peanut butter frosting decoratively over cupcakes.

Makes 22 cupcakes

Peanut Butter & Jelly Cupcakes

Red Velvet Cupcakes

2¼ cups all-purpose flour
1 teaspoon salt
2 bottles (1 ounce each) red food coloring
3 tablespoons unsweetened cocoa powder
1 cup buttermilk
1 teaspoon vanilla
1½ cups sugar
½ cup (1 stick) butter, softened
2 eggs
1 teaspoon white vinegar
1 teaspoon baking soda
1 to 2 containers (16 ounces each) whipped cream cheese frosting
Toasted coconut* (optional)

**To toast coconut, spread evenly on ungreased baking sheet. Bake in preheated 350°F oven 5 to 7 minutes or until light golden brown, stirring occasionally.*

1. Preheat oven to 350°F. Line 18 standard (2½-inch) muffin cups with paper baking cups.

2. Combine flour and salt in medium bowl. Gradually stir food coloring into cocoa in small bowl until blended and smooth. Combine buttermilk and vanilla in another small bowl.

3. Beat sugar and butter in large bowl with electric mixer at medium speed 4 minutes or until light and fluffy. Add eggs, one at a time, beating well after each addition. Add cocoa mixture; beat until well blended and uniform in color. Add flour mixture alternately with buttermilk mixture, beating just until blended. Stir vinegar into baking soda in small bowl; gently fold into batter with spatula or spoon (do not use mixer). Spoon batter into prepared muffin cups, filling two-thirds full.

4. Bake 18 to 20 minutes or until toothpick inserted into centers comes out clean. Cool cupcakes in pans 10 minutes; remove to wire racks to cool completely.

5. Generously spread frosting over cupcakes. Sprinkle with coconut, if desired.

Makes 18 cupcakes

Red Velvet Cupcakes

Black & Whites

1 package (about 18 ounces) vanilla cake mix, plus ingredients to prepare mix
⅔ cup semisweet chocolate chips, melted
4 ounces cream cheese, softened
1 cup prepared vanilla frosting
1 cup prepared chocolate frosting

1. Preheat oven to 350°F. Line 24 standard (2½-inch) muffin cups with paper baking cups.

2. Prepare cake mix according to package directions. Reserve half of batter (about 2½ cups) in medium bowl. Add melted chocolate and cream cheese to remaining batter; beat with electric mixer at medium speed about 2 minutes or until smooth and well blended.

3. Spoon chocolate and vanilla batters side by side into prepared muffin cups, filling about two-thirds full. (Use chocolate batter first as it is slightly thicker and easier to position on one side of muffin cups.)

4. Bake about 18 minutes or until toothpick inserted into centers comes out clean. Cool cupcakes in pans 10 minutes; remove to wire racks to cool completely.

5. Spread vanilla frosting over half of each cupcake; spread chocolate frosting over remaining half of each cupcake. *Makes 24 cupcakes*

Black & Whites

Mini Doughnut Cupcakes

- 1 cup sugar
- 1½ teaspoons ground cinnamon
- 1 package (about 18 ounces) yellow or white cake mix, plus ingredients to prepare mix
- 1 tablespoon ground nutmeg

1. Preheat oven to 350°F. Grease and flour 60 mini (1¾-inch) muffin cups. Combine sugar and cinnamon in small bowl; set aside.
2. Prepare cake mix according to package directions; stir in nutmeg. Spoon batter into prepared muffin cups, filling two-thirds full.
3. Bake 12 minutes or until lightly browned and toothpick inserted into centers comes out clean.
4. Remove cupcakes from pans. Roll warm cupcakes in sugar mixture until completely coated.

Makes 60 mini cupcakes

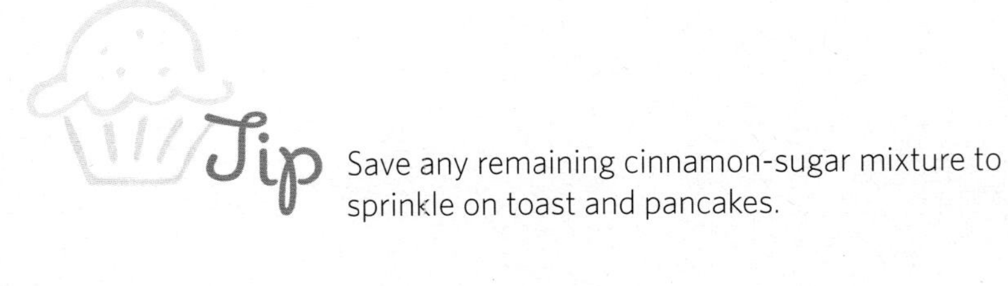

Tip Save any remaining cinnamon-sugar mixture to sprinkle on toast and pancakes.

Mini Doughnut Cupcakes

Chocolate Sweetheart Cupcakes

1 package (about 18 ounces) dark chocolate cake mix, plus ingredients to prepare mix
1 container (16 ounces) vanilla frosting
3 tablespoons seedless raspberry jam

1. Preheat oven to 350°F. Line 22 standard (2½-inch) muffin cups with paper baking cups.

2. Prepare cake mix according to package directions. Spoon batter into prepared muffin cups, filling two-thirds full.

3. Bake 18 to 20 minutes or until toothpick inserted into centers comes out clean. Cool cupcakes in pans 10 minutes; remove to wire racks to cool completely.

4. Blend frosting and jam in medium bowl until smooth. Cut off rounded tops of cupcakes with serrated knife. Cut out heart shape from each cupcake top with mini cookie cutter; reserve cutouts, if desired.

5. Spread frosting mixture generously over cupcake bottoms, mounding slightly in center. Replace cupcake tops, pressing gently to fill hearts with frosting mixture. Garnish with heart cutouts, if desired.

Makes 22 cupcakes

Tip Use the small hearts cut from the tops of these cupcakes to decorate cakes or additional cupcakes. Arrange the cutouts on top of white or colored frosting and sprinkle with powdered sugar, if desired.

Chocolate Sweetheart Cupcakes

Fruit Follies

Pink Lemonade Cupcakes

1 package (about 18 ounces) white cake mix without pudding in the mix
1 cup water
3 egg whites
⅓ cup plus ¼ cup thawed frozen pink lemonade concentrate, divided
2 tablespoons vegetable oil
5 to 8 drops red food coloring, divided
4 cups powdered sugar
⅓ cup butter, softened
Lemon slice candies (optional)

1. Preheat oven to 350°F. Line 24 standard (2½-inch) muffin cups with paper baking cups.

2. Beat cake mix, water, egg whites, ⅓ cup lemonade concentrate, oil and 4 to 6 drops food coloring in large bowl with electric mixer at medium speed 2 minutes or until well blended. Spoon batter evenly into prepared muffin cups.

3. Bake 18 to 22 minutes or until toothpick inserted into centers comes out clean. Cool cupcakes in pans 5 minutes; remove to wire racks to cool completely.

4. Beat powdered sugar, butter and remaining ¼ cup lemonade concentrate in medium bowl with electric mixer at medium speed until well blended. Beat in remaining 1 to 2 drops food coloring until desired shade of pink is reached.

5. Spread frosting over cupcakes. Garnish with candies and straws.

Makes 24 cupcakes

Banana Cupcakes

2 cups all-purpose flour
1½ cups granulated sugar
2 tablespoons packed brown sugar
2 teaspoons baking powder
½ teaspoon salt
½ teaspoon ground cinnamon
¼ teaspoon ground allspice
½ cup vegetable oil
2 eggs
¼ cup milk
1 teaspoon vanilla
2 mashed bananas (about 1 cup)
1 container (16 ounces) chocolate frosting
Chocolate sprinkles (optional)

1. Preheat cven to 350°F. Line 18 standard (2½-inch) muffin cups with paper baking cups.

2. Combine flour, granulated sugar, brown sugar, baking powder, salt, cinnamon and allspice in large bowl. Add oil, eggs, milk and vanilla; beat with electric mixer at medium speed 2 minutes or until well blended. Beat in bananas until well blended. Spoon batter into prepared muffin cups, filling three-fourths full.

3. Bake 25 to 30 minutes or until toothpick inserted into centers comes out clean. Cool cupcakes in pans 10 minutes; remove to wire racks to cool completely.

4. Frost cupcakes; decorate with sprinkles, if desired.

Makes 18 cupcakes

Banana Cupcakes

Key Lime Pie Cupcakes

1 package (about 18 ounces) lemon cake mix with pudding in the mix
1 cup vegetable oil
4 eggs
¾ cup key lime juice,* divided
½ cup water
1 teaspoon grated lime peel
2 cups whipping cream
½ cup powdered sugar
Lime wedges or additional grated lime peel (optional)

**If you cannot find key lime juice, substitute regular lime juice.*

1. Preheat oven to 350°F. Line 24 standard (2½-inch) muffin cups with paper baking cups.

2. Combine cake mix, oil, eggs, ½ cup key lime juice, water and lime peel in large bowl; whisk 2 minutes or until thick and smooth. Spoon batter into prepared muffin cups, filling two-thirds full.

3. Bake 19 to 23 minutes or until toothpick inserted into centers comes out clean. Cool cupcakes in pans 10 minutes; remove to wire racks to cool completely.

4. Beat cream in medium bowl with electric mixer at medium speed 3 to 5 minutes or until soft peaks form. Add sugar and remaining ¼ cup key lime juice; beat at medium-high speed 30 seconds or until medium-stiff peaks form. (Be careful not to overbeat or cream will break down.)

5. Top each cupcake with dollop of whipped cream. Garnish with lime wedges. Serve immediately.

Makes 24 cupcakes

Key Lime Pie Cupcakes

Strawberry Short Cupcakes

- 2 cups all-purpose flour
- 2½ teaspoons baking powder
- ½ teaspoon salt
- 1 cup milk
- 1 teaspoon vanilla
- 1½ cups plus 3 tablespoons sugar, divided
- ½ cup (1 stick) butter, softened
- 3 eggs
- 1½ cups cold whipping cream
- 2 quarts fresh strawberries, sliced

1. Preheat oven to 350°F. Spray 18 standard (2½-inch) muffin cups with nonstick cooking spray.

2. Combine flour, baking powder and salt in medium bowl. Combine milk and vanilla in small bowl. Beat 1½ cups sugar and butter in large bowl with electric mixer at medium speed about 3 minutes or until creamy. Add eggs, one at a time, beating well after each addition. Add flour mixture alternately with milk mixture, beating until well blended. Spoon batter into prepared muffin cups, filling about three-fourths full.

3. Bake 18 to 20 minutes or until toothpick inserted into centers comes out clean. Cool cupcakes in pans 10 minutes; remove to wire racks to cool completely.

4. Beat cream in large bowl with electric mixer at high speed until soft peaks form. Gradually add remaining 3 tablespoons sugar; beat until stiff peaks form.

5. Cut cupcakes in half crosswise. Top each bottom half with about 2 tablespoons whipped cream and strawberries. Replace top half; top with additional whipped cream and strawberries. *Makes 18 cupcakes*

Strawberry Short Cupcake

Lemon Meringue Cupcakes

1 package (about 18 ounces) lemon cake mix, plus ingredients to prepare mix
¾ cup prepared lemon curd*
4 egg whites, at room temperature
6 tablespoons sugar

**Lemon curd, a thick sweet lemon spread, is available in many supermarkets near the jams and preserves.*

1. Preheat oven to 350°F. Line 9 jumbo (3½-inch) muffin cups with paper baking cups.

2. Prepare cake mix according to package directions. Spoon batter into prepared muffin cups, filling two-thirds full.

3. Bake 23 to 25 minutes or until toothpick inserted into centers comes out clean. Cool cupcakes in pans 10 minutes; remove to wire racks to cool completely. *Increase oven temperature to 375°F.*

4. Cut off tops of cupcakes with serrated knife. (Do not remove paper baking cups.) Scoop out small hole in center of each cupcake with tablespoon; fill hole with generous tablespoon lemon curd. Replace cupcake tops.

5. Beat egg whites in medium bowl with electric mixer at high speed until soft peaks form. Continue beating while gradually adding sugar; beat until stiff peaks form. Pipe or spread meringue in peaks on each cupcake.

6. Place cupcakes on baking sheet. Bake 5 to 6 minutes or until peaks of meringue are golden.

Makes 9 jumbo cupcakes

Variation: This recipe also makes 22 standard (2½-inch) cupcakes. Line muffin pans with paper baking cups; prepare and bake cake mix according to package directions. Cut off tops of cupcakes; scoop out hole in each cupcake with teaspoon and fill with generous teaspoon lemon curd. Replace tops and pipe or spread about ⅓ cup meringue in peaks on each cupcake; bake as directed above.

Lemon Meringue Cupcakes

Blueberry Cheesecake Cupcakes

- 1 package (16 ounces) refrigerated mini break-apart sugar cookie dough
- 2 packages (8 ounces each) cream cheese, softened
- 1 cup sugar
- 2 eggs
- 1 tablespoon cornstarch
- 1½ teaspoons vanilla
- 3 egg whites
- ½ teaspoon cream of tartar
- ¼ cup blueberry preserves
- 1 pint fresh blueberries (optional)

1. Preheat oven to 325°F. Line 20 standard (2½-inch) muffin cups with foil baking cups; lightly spray with nonstick cooking spray.

2. Break off 2 cookie pieces from cookie dough. Roll into a ball, flatten slightly and press into bottom of baking cup. Repeat with remaining dough. Bake 10 minutes; immediately press down center of each crust with back of spoon to flatten.

3. Beat cream cheese in large bowl with electric mixer at medium speed until smooth. Add sugar, eggs, cornstarch and vanilla; beat until smooth and well blended.

4. Beat egg whites and cream of tartar in medium bowl with electric mixer at high speed until stiff peaks form. Stir half of egg white mixture into cream cheese mixture. Gently fold in remaining egg white mixture just until combined. Swirl in blueberry preserves. *Do not overmix.* Spoon batter over cooled cookie crusts.

5. Bake 17 to 20 minutes. (Centers will be spongy to the touch). Cool cupcakes in pans 10 minutes; place pans in refrigerator to cool completely. Remove from pans; store in airtight container until ready to serve. Garnish with blueberries.

Makes 20 cupcakes

Note: It is important to use foil baking cups because they provide extra structure for the cheesecake.

Blueberry Cheesecake Cupcake

Raspberry Streusel Cupcakes

Streusel Topping (recipe follows)
3 cups all-purpose flour
2 teaspoons baking powder
½ teaspoon salt
⅛ teaspoon ground cinnamon
1½ cups sugar
½ cup (1 stick) butter, softened
2 eggs
1 teaspoon vanilla
1 cup sour cream
1½ pints fresh raspberries

1. Preheat oven to 350°F. Line 24 standard (2½-inch) muffin cups with paper baking cups. Prepare Streusel Topping; set aside.

2. Whisk flour, baking powder, salt and cinnamon in medium bowl. Beat sugar and butter in large bowl with electric mixer at medium speed 2 to 3 minutes or until light and fluffy. Add eggs, one at a time, beating well after each addition. Stir in vanilla. Add flour mixture alternately with sour cream, beating just until blended. Gently fold in raspberries. Spoon evenly into prepared muffin cups; sprinkle with Streusel Topping.

3. Bake 20 to 25 minutes or until toothpick inserted into centers comes out clean. Cool cupcakes in pans 10 minutes; remove to wire racks to cool completely. *Makes 24 cupcakes*

Streusel Topping: Combine 1 cup sugar, ⅔ cup all-purpose flour, ¼ cup pecan chips, 1 teaspoon ground cinnamon and ¼ teaspoon salt in medium bowl. Cut ½ cup (1 stick) butter into small pieces; cut butter and 1 tablespoon milk into sugar mixture with pastry blender or two knives until mixture resembles coarse crumbs.

Raspberry Streusel Cupcakes